TOFU NOW

A National Organization for Women Cookbook

Want some TOFU in your diet
Not a vegetarian
Not a gourmet
This is the cookbook for you

by Susan Lebow

Best wishes
eat healthy
Susan Lebow

TOFU NOW
by Susan Lebow

Published by: National Organization for Women, Inc.
733 15th Street NW, 2nd Floor
Washington, DC 20005

Order at www.now.org/catalog

Acknowledgements:
I am ever great-full to my husband Richard Dean for cordially eating every one of my experiments, and contributing invaluably to this cookbook.
To Connie Beals, my wonder-full and witty counsel.
And to Trade Printery, the oldest woman owned and run Union shop in Seattle Washington for their unsolicited generosity to NOW.

Cover Art: by Anne Gordon

Library of Congress Control Number: 2004100300

ISBN: 0-9638563-7-5

Printed in the United States of America on recycled paper

First Printing: 2004

I wrote this cookbook to honor the best cook I know
my mom Lorraine Lebow

Table of Contents

Tofu is soybean curd - the cheese made from soy milk. It's high octane - easy to digest - clean burning - complete vegetable protein - with all the essential amino acids - plenty of vitamin B - and zero cholesterol.

TOFU NOW will teach you how to handle this wonder-full bean curd just as if you were using meat. After you've read pages 1 and 2 - and have tried a few recipes from each category - you and the bean curd will already be old friends.

A few things to keep in mind:
— if you think of tofu as the meat you would use in the same dish - it begins to make sense. And just like meat - tofu is more appealing when cooked.
— any brand will do. You'll soon find your own favorite.
— make sure it's fresh - <u>look at the expiration date</u> - the fresher the better. Tofu has a barely noticeable mild sort of nutty aroma when fresh. You'll have no problem knowing when it's spoiled - no more than you would spoiled meat. If the tofu you've just bought smells sour when opened - is slimy - or looks frothy or pinkish - it's already spoiled. Take it back. We buy where the store knows enough to keep their tofu in the refrigerated section - not just with the vegetables.
— <u>when frozen tofu is called for **do not** substitute fresh</u>.
— tofu takes on the flavor of what ever you add to it.
— it may seem we're calling for way too much flavorings – herbs and spices - but our rule of thumb is - twice as much as you would if you were cooking meat.
— it's a good idea to read each recipe completely before beginning.

Types of Tofu:
— the firmness and texture of the tofu makes all the difference to the outcome of your dish. <u>We will tell you in each recipe what type to use and how to use it.</u>
— **extra-firm**: good on the bar-b-que - we rarely use it for anything else.
— **firm**: great for frying - grilling - in certain sandwiches - and for crumbling.
— **regular to firm:** the type we use most - for stir-fry - hearty soups and stews - sandwiches - casseroles.
— **soft**: for some soups and scrambled eggs.
— **silken tofu**: whether extra-firm or soft - is very delicate and creamy smooth - and we only use it for soups and sauces.

Purchasing and Storage:
— tofu is usually sold in one pound (16oz.) portions. If your package is 14 to 19 ounces - treat it as if it were one pound.
— fresh tofu if vacuum sealed can stay unopened in the refrigerator for two weeks. Check the expiration date.
— otherwise - fresh tofu should be rinsed when you bring it home - and stored covered in cold water in the refrigerator. You can keep it up to two weeks if you change the water daily.
— if you don't use the tofu - regular and firm only - by the expiration time - no problem - freeze it. We always like to keep some frozen tofu on hand.

Freezing:
— only freeze regular and firm tofu - never soft or silken.
— tofu that's been frozen for at least 24 hours is essential to the recipes that call for frozen.
— freezing tofu alters the texture - making it meatier - more absorbent - and looking like a sponge - and don't worry if the color has changed to a yellowish tan - it disappears after thawing.
— vacuum-sealed fresh tofu can be frozen as-is for three months.
— if not vacuum sealed - gently pat the block with paper towels - and double-wrap tightly in plastic before freezing.

To Thaw:
— when a recipe calls for frozen tofu - we put it in the microwave as soon as we get home.
— all frozen tofu recipes are timed for a 20 minute microwave defrost
— place the frozen tofu in a microwave safe bowl - make a hole in the plastic — use the defrost setting - 10 to 25 minutes depending on the power of your microwave - till the tofu is thawed all the way through.
— or you can place the frozen tofu in a bowl of hot tap water till thawed all the way through. This takes an hour or more.
— or leave it overnight in the frig.
— once thawed - gently squeeze out the water. We put it between the backs of two plates and apply gentle even pressure. Some people prefer to use their hands. Either way be gentle.

- tsp.   = teaspoon
- Tbls. = tablespoon

Basic everyday tofu

Scrambled eggs - simple or deluxe

A hearty easy meal any time. For breakfast serve **simple scramble** on buttered English muffins with plenty of ketchup. Lunch - try **deluxe #1** piled on whole wheat toast. And as a get-home-late meal - **deluxe #2** spooned into warm burrito shells and smothered with your favorite salsa.
Serves: 2 - 3 - you can cut ingredients in half for 1 person
Prep time: 10 minutes
Cooking time: 5 minutes for simple - 10 minutes for deluxe #1 or #2

Ingredients for simple scramble:
- 1/2 pound **regular tofu - fresh**
- 3 large eggs
- 1/4 to 1/2 tsp.salt
- 1 tsp.onion powder
- 1/8 tsp.black pepper
- 1 1/2 Tbls.oil - we prefer canola or olive

How to - simple scramble:
- place tofu in a 2 quart mixing bowl and crumble with
  a large fork into olive size pieces
- break eggs into the same bowl
- add all the spices and beat to break up eggs and blend
- pour oil into a 12" fry pan - turn burner to high
- add tofu mixture - turn burner down to medium and
  scramble till firm - about 5 minutes

Additions to simple scramble for deluxe #1:
- 3 scallions sliced very thin
- 4 oz.can sliced mushrooms - well drained
- 1/4 tsp.garlic powder
- 1/2 cup grated cheddar or jack cheese
How to - deluxe #1:
- in a 12" fry pan - sauté scallions and
  mushrooms in 1 1/2 Tbls.oil on medium - 5 minutes
- now follow simple scramble - adding garlic powder to
  the spices and leaving out any more oil
- when eggs are set - sprinkle with cheese and serve

Additions to simple scramble for deluxe #2:
- one 4 oz.can diced chilies - well drained
- 1/4 tsp.garlic powder
- 1/2 cup grated cheddar or jack cheese
- your favorite salsa - if you're feeling ambitious try
  the recipe on p.54
How to - deluxe #2:
- mix chilies in with tofu and eggs
- add garlic powder to simple scramble spices
- cook in a 12" fry pan as directed
- when set - top with cheese and salsa and serve.

Breaded cutlets

This is a savory main dish served with rice and vegetables - and also makes for delicious sandwiches - hot or cold.
Serves: 2 - 3
Prep time: 10 minutes
Cooking time: 25 minutes

Ingredients:
- one pound **regular or firm tofu - fresh**
- 1 package any flavor dry mix - gravy - burrito -
  fajitas - sloppy joe - beef stew - soup or meat marinade
  - just do not use spaghetti sauce - noodle or vegetable soup mix
- 1 heaping Tbls.white flour - we use Wondera here
- 2 tsp.onion powder
- 1/4 to 1/2 tsp.salt
- 3 Tbls.oil - we prefer corn here

How to:
- slice tofu into 5 equal slabs - then slice them across
  making 10 squares
- pour your choice packaged mix - flour - onion powder and
  salt into a soup bowl and blend well with a fork or whisk
- carefully coat each cutlet on all sides and set on a plate
- heat 2 Tbls.oil on medium in a 12" frying pan
- lay in the cutlets - being careful not to break them
- fry 5 minutes
- add 1 more Tbls.oil to pan - turn cutlets over carefully
  and fry 5 minutes
- add 3/4 cup water to pan - turn burner to medium-low and
  simmer till all the liquid is gone - about 15 minutes.

Charcoal grilled bar-b-que ribs

You can also grill any color bell peppers and onions cut in quarters – even whole scallions are great on the grill – zucchini sliced in half the long way – whole large mushrooms – husked corn broken in half – any veggies in season – just marinate – and lay them right on the grill with the tofu. We love garlic French bread with this finger lickin' feast. Or you can skip the veggies and go right to sandwiches – just use any very fresh bread – we recommend potato.

Serves: 2 – 3
Prep time: 10 minutes + 20 minutes defrost – refer to p.2
Grilling time: 30 minutes

Ingredients:
- one pound **firm tofu – frozen and thawed**
- **marinate #1:**
  - your favorite bottle of bar-b-que sauce – we prefer honeyed
  - *optional – if not honeyed – add 3 Tbls.honey or 2 Tbls.molasses*
  - 3 Tbls.oil – we like olive or canola here
  - *optional – 1/4 cup wine or beer*
- **marinate #2:**
  - 3/4 cup oil – we like olive or canola here
  - 1/2 tsp.garlic powder – not garlic salt
  - 2 tsp.onion powder – not onion salt
  - 1/4 tsp.pepper – fresh cracked
  - 1 heaping Tbls.mild yellow mustard
  - *optional - 1/4 cup wine or beer*
  - *optional - 1 tsp.Worcestershire and/or 1 Tbls.soy sauce*
  - *optional - 1/4 to 1 tsp.hot sauce - we use 1/2 tsp.*

How to:
- squeeze thawed tofu well - refer to thaw p.2
- pat dry with paper towels
- slice into 5 equal slabs
- place in a 7x11 glass baking dish
- marinate #1 or #2:
  - whisk ingredients together in order till well
    blended - *we like to add all the optionals*
- pour over tofu and let stand 1 minute - that's all
- remove to a platter
- if you're grilling veggies - dip them in marinade and
  place on platter with tofu
- pour the remaining marinate in a bowl for basting
- lay tofu and veggies on hot grill
- grill till very browned - even burnt which is our favorite
- baste just once before turning
- and turn one time only.

Chicken morsels

Use these tasty nuggets hot or cold in the same way you would chicken - to stuff pita bread - tacos or burritos - hot over rice or pasta - even cold in a salad.
Serves: 2 - 3
Prep time: 10 minutes
Cooking time: 30 minutes

Ingredients:
- one pound **firm tofu - fresh**
- 2 Tbls.oil - we prefer corn or canola here
- 1/4 to 1/2 tsp.salt
- 1 tsp.onion powder - not onion salt
- 1/8 tsp.pepper - fresh cracked is best
- 2 vegetable or chicken bouillon cube <u>or</u> 1 heaping tsp.granules <u>or</u>
  one Knorr bouillon cube - we prefer Knorr but any brand will do
- 1 Tbls.soy sauce - we use tamari

How to:
- slice tofu into 5 equal slabs - cut those in half
  lengthwise - and cut each into 4 chunks
- pour oil into a 10" fry pan
- add tofu
- sprinkle evenly with salt - onion powder and pepper
- sauté 10 minutes on medium - browning chunks on all
  sides - use a wooden spoon to turn - gently
  so as not to break them
- dissolve bouillon in 1/2 cup boiling water - add soy sauce
  and pour slowly into fry pan
- simmer uncovered on medium-low till all the liquid is
  gone - about 20 minutes.

Hamburger nut patties

These are moist and satisfying. Use them hot for burgers - or with mashed potatoes and veggies smothered in gravy - or serve them cold the next day in sandwiches.
Serves: 4 - with leftovers
Prep time: 10 minutes
Cooking time: 40 minutes

Ingredients:
- one pound **regular tofu - fresh**
- 1 large egg
- 1 tsp.Worcestershire sauce <u>or</u> 1 Tbls.soy sauce
- 1/2 cup quick oatmeal - unflavored
- 2 Tbls.white flour - we use Wondera here
- 1 Tbls.corn starch
- *optionals - 1 Tbls.wheat germ and/or 1 Tbls.lecithin*
- 1/2 cup crushed walnuts - we put the nuts in a plastic bag
  and roll over them with a rolling pin till crushed
- 2 tsp.dry soup granules - beef flavor - we use Knorr but any brand is fine
- 1/4 to 1/2 tsp.salt
- 1/8 tsp.pepper
- 1 Tbls.onion powder - not onion salt
- 1/2 tsp.garlic powder - not garlic salt
- 1/2 tsp.oregano - Mexican if you have it
- 1/2 tsp.sweet basil
- 4 Tbls.oil - we prefer corn but any vegetable oil will do

How to:
- pat tofu dry with paper towels
- place in a 2 quart mixing bowl
- mash with a large fork to the appearance of cottage cheese
- add egg and Worcestershire <u>or</u> soy sauce and beat maybe
  ten strokes - till egg is well distributed
- in another bowl combine - oatmeal - flour - cornstarch
  - *optionals* - nuts - soup granules and all the spices
- sprinkle evenly over tofu and mix well
- form into 8 patties and lay on a plate
- heat 1 Tbls.oil in a 12" frying pan on medium-high
- add 4 patties and fry to very brown and crisp - about 10 minutes
- add 1 Tbls.oil to pan - turn patties over and brown well
- repeat with the remaining patties.

Oven bar-b-que ribs

These are great in the winter when you hanker for a sunny summer meal. Serve with baked potatoes and salad. Or we love them as a hot sandwich - on potato bread or a Kaiser roll - just make sure the bread is fresh so it can soak-up the delicious sauce.

Serves: 2 - 3
Prep time: 10 minutes + 20 minutes defrost - refer to p.2
Baking time: 45 minutes

Ingredients:
- one pound **regular or firm tofu - frozen and thawed**
- **Sauce**:
    - your favorite bottle of bar-b-que sauce - we prefer honeyed
    - *optional - if not honeyed - add 3 Tbls.honey or 1 Tbls.molasses*
    - 2 Tbls.oil or butter - your choice - we prefer walnut oil
      or melted butter here
    - 1/4 tsp.garlic powder - not garlic salt
    - 1 tsp.onion powder - not onion salt
    - *optional - 1/4 tsp.ground cinnamon*
    - *optional - 1 Tbls.soy sauce*
    - *optional - 2 Tbls.wine or beer*

How to:
- turn your oven to 350°
- squeeze thawed tofu well - refer to thaw p.2
- pat with paper towels
- cut in 5 equal slabs - and cut those in half lengthwise
- place in a 9x11 baking pan - we prefer glass
- mix sauce in bowl with whisk - *we add all of the optionals*
- pour over tofu
- bake uncovered - 45 minutes - turning only once - till well
  browned - even burnt.

Baked onion burgers

These make for a remarkable sandwich with all the fixings.
Serves: 3
Prep time: 10 minutes + 20 minutes defrost - refer to p.2
Baking time: 50 minutes

Ingredients:
- one pound **regular or firm tofu - frozen and thawed**
- one package dry onion <u>or</u> onion-mushroom soup mix
- 2 Tbls.oil - any vegetable oil will do - we use canola here
- 3 Tbls.soy sauce - we prefer tamari
- 1 Tbls.roasted sesame seeds - you can do this yourself by
  putting the seeds in a dry fry pan on medium heat and
  stirring often till browned - about 5 minutes
- 1/2 to 1 tsp.hot sauce - we prefer Trappey's mexi-pep
- 1/4 to 1/2 tsp.salt
- 1/4 tsp.garlic powder - not garlic salt
- 1/2 tsp.onion powder - not onion salt
- 1/8 tsp.pepper - we like fresh cracked
- hamburger buns or fresh bread
- your choice of fixings - mayo - ketchup - relish - lettuce
  - tomato - pickles - thin sliced onion - cheddar cheese

How to:
- squeeze thawed tofu well - refer to thaw p.2
- slice into 6 equal slabs
- pour oil into an 8x11 glass baking dish
- lay in tofu
- turn oven to 325°
- sprinkle tofu evenly with salt - garlic and onion powder -
  pepper - and sesame seeds
- sprinkle soup mix evenly over and pat down with fork
  to break up any lumps
- in a small bowl - mix soy sauce - hot sauce and 1 cup water
- pour over tofu and bake uncovered till the liquid has
  evaporated - about 50 minutes
- now build yourself a burger - your way.

Reuben sandwich

For those who love a Jewish deli - serve with kosher dill pickles and sliced tomatoes on the side.
Serves: 3 big satisfying sandwiches
Prep time: 15 minutes + 20 minutes defrost - refer to p.2
Cooking time: 45 minutes

Ingredients:
- one pound **regular tofu - frozen and thawed**
- 2 Tbls.fat - canola or corn oil - or butter - or margarine
  - we use non-hydrogenated margarine with no trans-fatty acids
- 1 package dry soup mix - onion-mushroom or beefy-onion
- bread - we like fresh rye here - but you can use sourdough
  cracked wheat - or any kind as long as it's really fresh
- mayonnaise
- spicy brown mustard
- sauerkraut - jar or can - we prefer the jar
- *optional - creamy mild horseradish*
- Swiss cheese - or any white cheese - no cheddar

How to:
- squeeze tofu well - refer to thaw p.2
- pat dry with paper towel
- slice into six equal slabs
- pour fat into a 12" frying pan
- lay in tofu
- sprinkle soup mix evenly over top and pat down with a
  fork to break-up any lumps
- pour in 1 cup water - we prefer filtered water
- bring to a boil - turn down and simmer uncovered - turning
  the tofu once - till all the liquid is gone but tofu is
  not dried-out - about 45 minutes
- spread mayo on all bread slices
- mustard on half the slices - we use lots
- squeeze 1/3 cup sauerkraut dry in paper towels for each sandwich
- place the kraut on the mustard slice
- lay two pieces of tofu on the kraut - this will warm it up
- *spread 1/2 tsp.horseradish on tofu*
- place thin sliced cheese over horseradish
- cover with the other slice of bread and cut in half.

American

Macaroni & cheese bake

The ultimate comfort food. And not such a guilty pleasure made with tofu.
Serves: 3 - 4
Prep time: 20 minutes
Baking time: 20 minutes

Ingredients:
- one pound **regular tofu - fresh**
- 2 cups dry macaroni noodles or shells
- 3 Tbls.butter or margarine - if you use margarine - try
  the non-hydrogenated kind that has no trans-fatty acids
- 3/4 cup dry bread crumbs - you can make these yourself buy
  chopping-up 2 slices of bread and baking them on a
  cookie sheet at 250° for 1/2 hour
- 1 1/2 cup milk - skim or whole
- 1 pound cheddar cheese - grated - we like American
  cheddar here or Velveeta
- onion powder - not onion salt
- salt
- pepper
- *optional dry mustard*
- one large tomato

How to:
- cook noodles according to package
- rinse and drain in strainer
- grease a large glass or ceramic casserole with 1 Tbls.
  butter and pour in noodles
- turn oven to 400°
- melt 1 Tbls.butter in medium size sauce pan
- pour in bread crumbs - toss - and set aside in a bowl
- in same sauce pan - melt 1 Tbls.butter on low
- add milk and blend with a whisk
- add 1 tsp.onion powder - 1/4 to 1/2 tsp.salt - 1/8 tsp.pepper
  - 1/4 tsp.dry mustard - and blend
- add cheese 1/2 cup at a time - blend smooth after each -
  then remove from burner
- pat tofu with a paper towel - place in a medium size bowl
  and crumble with a fork into cottage cheese size pieces
- mix into noodles
- pour sauce over and mix till noodles and tofu are coated
- cut tomato into thin rounds and lay on top in a circle
- spoon on bread crumbs evenly
- bake uncovered - 20 minutes.

Potato salad

This is a creamy saucy whole meal in itself without all the mayo. And a great take-with-you to someone's house - to turn them on to tofu.
Serves: 4 to 8 depending if it's a main or side dish
Prep time: 30 minutes + 3 hours chill time
Cooking time: 15 minutes

Ingredients:
- 8-10 oz.**firm silken tofu - fresh**
- 4 large to jumbo eggs - if medium or small use 6
- 3 large russet baking potatoes – we like Idaho
- *optional - 1 large onion - Walla Walla - Bermuda - taste first - make sure it's mild and sweet - or leave out*
- 3 stalks celery - we use the tender inner stalks
- 4 scallions
- *optional - 20 green olives with pimento*
- 1/2 cup mayonnaise
- 1 heaping Tbls.mild yellow mustard
- 1/4 cup sweet pickle relish
- 2 tsp.lemon juice
- 1 tsp.sugar
- salt - we prefer natural sea salt - and coarse kosher sea salt for garnish
- pepper - we use fresh cracked here

How to:
- boil eggs 11–13 minutes in water with 1 tsp.salt - shell immediately and set aside in cold water
- skin potatoes - cut into 1/2 inch cubes
- boil potatoes in egg water – 10 minutes
- pour potatoes into a strainer - and let drain
- combine in a large bowl
    - *finely chop mild sweet onion*
    - finely chop celery
    - and scallions sliced very thin using whites and greens
    - add the potatoes
    - mix gently with a big wooden spoon once or twice
- in a separate bowl
    - mash tofu with a big fork or pastry blender
    - add mayo - mustard - relish - lemon juice - sugar – 1/4 to 1/2 tsp.salt – and 1/4 tsp.pepper
    - whip with a whisk till very smooth
- pour this over potatoes and vegetables - mix only to coat
- cut eggs into eighths *and green olives in half* - and add
- mix for the last time - just enough to distribute ingredients evenly
- here we like to sprinkle the top with coarse kosher sea salt and more fresh cracked black pepper
- cover and refrigerate at least 3 hours.

Honeyed ham sandwich

These cutlets are delicious all by themselves on very fresh whole wheat bread - or add red leaf lettuce and lots of mayo. Out of lettuce - open a can of string beans - rinse and drain - lay on paper towels to dry - and use instead. These cutlets also makes for a great cold sandwich - with spicy brown mustard - cheddar cheese and a thin slice of purple onion.

Serves: 2 - 3
Prep time: 10 minutes + 20 minutes defrost - refer to p.2
Cooking time: 45 minutes

Ingredients:
- one pound **regular tofu - frozen and thawed**
- 2 Tbls.oil - we like canola but any vegetable oil is fine
- 1/4 to 1/2 tsp.salt
- 1/8 tsp.pepper - we like white pepper here
- 1 tsp.onion powder - not onion salt
- 1/4 tsp.five spice - this is the magic ingredient - do not leave it out
- 1/4 cup honey
- 2 Tbls.soy sauce - we use tamari
- one 8 oz.can pineapple chunks in heavy syrup

How to:
- squeeze thawed tofu well - refer to thaw p.2
- pat dry with paper towels
- slice into 6 equal slabs
- pour oil in a 12" frying pan
- lay in tofu
- sprinkle spices evenly on slabs
- drizzle honey liberally over all
- add soy sauce
- pour in pineapple and juice
- bring to a boil - turn to low and simmer covered for 10 minutes
- then turn stove up to low-medium - flip cutlets over
  and continue cooking uncovered till all liquid is gone
  - about 30 minutes
- let cool 5 minutes - then build yourself a ham sandwich.

Kasha pilaf - as a main dish

Kasha is a wonderful nutty flavored whole grain alternative to rice. It's buckwheat groats - and more Russian than American - but then combining tofu and buckwheat happened in an American kitchen - so we placed it in this category. You can serve this dish with a green salad and tomato soup if you want a bigger meal.

Serves: 2 - 3
Prep time: 30 minutes
Cooking time: 30 minutes

Ingredients:
- one pound **regular tofu - fresh**
- 1 cup roasted kasha
- 1 egg - any size
- 3 Tbls.oil - olive - walnut or canola - we prefer walnut
- 1 large yellow onion
- 1/2 pound fresh mushrooms - or one 4 oz.can - well drained
- 1/3 cup broken walnuts - pecans are good too
- 2 cups hot broth - made from beef or vegetable bouillon
  cubes or granules - we like Knorr but any brand is fine
- salt
- pepper - fresh cracked if you have it

How to:
- in a 1 quart bowl - mix kasha groats and egg with a
  fork till all the groats are coated
- pour 1 Tbls.oil into a deep 12" frying pan
- cook groats over medium heat stirring constantly with a
  wooden spoon - till brown and separated - 5 minutes
- put kasha in bowl and set aside for now
- add 1 Tbls.oil to the same fry pan on medium heat
- chop onion - and brown it well - this makes for
  lots of meaty flavor - about 10 minutes
- add onions to kasha on the side
- cut tofu into 5 equal slabs - cut lengthwise into
  three equal fingers - and cut each of those across five times
- slice mushrooms thickish
- add 1 Tbls.oil to the same frying pan and sauté tofu and
  mushrooms over medium heat uncovered - 10 minutes -
  stirring every few minutes gently with a wooden spoon
- add kasha - onion - nuts - and broth
- sprinkle on 1/4 to 1/2 tsp.salt and 1/8 tsp.pepper
- mix gently to distribute ingredients
- bring to a boil - turn down to low
- cover tightly and simmer 30 minutes - till all the liquid has been absorbed.

Crispy red potato bake

This easy dish is a winner. Serve with steamed vegetables and a good hot mustard on the side.
Serves: 2 - 3
Prep time: 10 minutes
Baking time: 60 minutes

Ingredients:
- one pound **firm tofu - fresh**
- 1 package dry gravy mix - beef - chicken - turkey
- country - your choice - any brand is fine
- 2 Tbls.white flour - we use Wondera here
- 4 good size red potatoes
- 1/4 cup oil - use what you have - but we definitely prefer olive
- 1/4 to 1/2 tsp.salt - we like sea salt for all those good minerals
- 1/4 tsp.pepper - fresh cracked
- 2 tsp.onion powder - not onion salt
- 1/2 tsp.garlic powder - not garlic salt
- 1/3 cup grated parmesan cheese

How to:
- turn oven to 325°
- pat tofu dry with paper towels - cut into 4 equal slabs
  - cut those lengthwise - and cut each length into 4 cubes
- using a whisk - blend gravy mix and flour together in
  a 2 quart mixing bowl - *if using country gravy reduce flour to 1 Tbls.
- add tofu and toss gently to coat
- pour oil over the bottom of a 11x16 aluminum baking pan
- add tofu and turn each piece once to coat with oil
- scrub potatoes - pat dry - cut off any spots and eyes
- quarter each potato - coat <u>one</u> cut side with gravy
  mix - and place that side down in baking pan
- take a pastry brush and using oil from the pan - coat the
  potato skins - you may need more oil
- sprinkle evenly with salt - pepper - onion and garlic powders
- bake 35 minutes uncovered - without turning
- sprinkle with parmesan - bake 25 minutes more.

Stroganoff noodles

Satisfying comfort food. You can open a can of string beans with this - or make some frozen vegetables or a green salad - or just spoon the noodles into a bowl and enjoy.
Serves: 2 - with some leftover
Prep time: 30 minutes
Baking time: 40 minutes

Ingredients:
- one pound **regular tofu - fresh**
- fat - canola or corn oil <u>and</u> butter or margarine - if it's margarine
  - we recommend the non-hydrogenated with no trans-fatty acids
- 1/4 tsp.garlic powder - not garlic salt
- 2 tsp.onion powder - not onion salt
- 1/8 tsp.pepper - we prefer fresh cracked
- 1 package dry soup mix - onion-mushroom <u>or</u> beefy-onion
- 1 large yellow onion
- 3/4 pound fresh mushrooms <u>or</u> one 8 oz.can - well drained
- 2 cups dry noodles - we prefer egg ribbons - but small shells will do
- 1 can cream of mushroom soup - regular or low fat
- 3/4 cup milk - whole or skim
- 1/2 to 1 cup sour cream - regular or lite

How to:
- slice tofu in 6 equal slabs - and quarter each of those
- place 2 Tbls.oil in a deep 12" frying pan
- lay in the tofu carefully so as not to break
- sprinkle with garlic and onion powder - and pepper
- then sprinkle on soup mix evenly and pat down with a fork
  to break-up any lumps
- slice mushrooms thickish and lay on top
- cut onion into 8 wedges and lay over mushrooms
- pour in 1/2 cup water - we prefer filtered
- bring to a boil - cover tightly - turn down and simmer - 20 minutes
- now - cook noodles according to the package and drain well
- grease - we prefer 1 Tbls.butter here - a glass or ceramic
  casserole or 9x12 baking dish
- turn oven to 350°
- pour noodles evenly into dish or casserole
- using a spatula - spoon tofu mixture over noodles
  along with all the good pan juices
- mix mushroom soup with milk - leave it sort of lumpy
- pour evenly over noodles
- dot with sour cream
- cover with tin foil and bake 25 minutes.

Stuffing - as a main dish

Serve with your favorite Thanksgiving fixings - cranberry sauce - green beans - maybe a salad - and canned or packaged gravy if you like - although the stuffing is quite moist and really doesn't need it. If there's any leftover - we like cold stuffing sandwiches the next day - just like turkey.

Serves: 2-3 as a main dish - 4 as a side
Prep time: 60 minutes
Baking time: 50 minutes

Ingredients:
- one pound **regular tofu - fresh**
- fat - we prefer walnut oil <u>and</u> butter here - but you can use any vegetable oil and margarine if you must
- 1 large yellow onion
- 1/2 pound fresh mushrooms sliced thin - <u>or</u> one 4 oz.can sliced - well drained
- one package dry soup mix - onion <u>or</u> onion-mushroom
- *optional - two medium red potatoes*
- one 12-16 oz.bag or box of dry seasoned stuffing
- *optional - 2 stalks celery - the tender inside stalks*
- 1/2 cup chopped nuts - pistachio - macadamia - pecans - walnuts - almonds - any kind but peanuts
- 1/2 cup dark raisins
- parsley - dry or fresh chopped
- rosemary - <u>or</u> ground cumin - <u>or</u> sage - we prefer rosemary
- salt
- pepper
- garlic powder - not garlic salt
- onion powder - not onion salt
- *optional - one 4 oz.can sliced water chestnuts - well drained*
- *optional - 1 apple - we prefer a Rome beauty*
- 1 cube chicken <u>or</u> vegetable bouillon - dissolved in one cup boiling water - we use Knorr but any brand will do

How To:
- pour 1 Tbls.oil in a deep 12" frying pan and turn
  burner to medium
- chop onion and add - cook till brown but not burnt
  - about 10 minutes
- slice tofu into 7 equal slabs - cut each slab into 1/2" cubes
- add tofu to onion
- lay mushrooms over tofu
- sprinkle soup mix evenly over - pat down with fork
  to break-up any lumps
- add 1 cup water - we like filtered
- bring to a boil - turn down - cover - simmer 30 minutes
- *while that's cooking - bake potatoes - 425° - 30 minutes*
- now - in a very large bowl
- pour dry stuffing - and packaged seasoning if separate
- *chop celery very thin and add*
- chop nuts and add - we crush them in a plastic bag with a
  rolling pin - or you can buy them already chopped
- add raisins
- and parsley - 1 tsp.dry or 1/4 cup fresh chopped
- sprinkle on 1 tsp.rosemary - <u>or</u> 1/2 tsp.cumin - <u>or</u> 1/2 tsp.sage
- 1/4 to 1/2 tsp.salt
- 1/8 tsp.pepper
- 1/2 tsp.garlic powder
- and 2 tsp.onion powder
- mix well with a large wooden spoon
- *when potatoes are done - remove* - turn oven to 350°
- *add water chestnuts <u>and/or</u> chopped apple to stuffing*
- pour bouillon over all
- drizzle on 1/4 cup melted butter <u>or</u> margarine and mix
- *skin and slice potatoes thin - mix in gently*
- using a spatula - add tofu and every bit of the yummy
  sauce from the pan
- mix again gently so as not to break-up the tofu
- grease a large casserole dish or 9x13 baking pan with
  1 Tbls.butter
- spoon in the stuffing - do not pack down
- bake covered with tin foil - 40 minutes
- uncover 10 minutes to brown.

Meat loaf

This is wonderful served on a platter surrounded with mashed potatoes and steamed vegetables. And just as good left over the next day on a sandwich with lots of ketchup or mustard.

Servings: 4
Prep time: 45 minutes
Baking time: 60 minutes

Ingredients:
- one pound **soft tofu - fresh**
- 2 cups dry brown lentils - rinsed in a strainer
- 1 bay leaf
- 1 large yellow onion
- fat - canola - corn or olive oil - <u>and</u> some butter
- 2 slices bread - use what ever you have on hand
- 1/4 cup potato flakes <u>or</u> unflavored quick oats
- 1/2 tsp.oregano - we prefer Mexican
- 1/2 tsp.ground cumin
- 1 Tbls.onion powder - not onion salt
- 1/2 tsp.garlic powder - not garlic salt
- 1/8 tsp.pepper
- salt – we use sea salt for all the good minerals
- 1 package dry soup mix - onion-mushroom <u>or</u> beefy-onion
- 1 large or 2 small eggs
- 1/3 cup ground walnuts
- ketchup

How to:
- bring lentils to a boil in 6 cups water and 1/2 tsp.salt
- *add bay leaf* - turn down - cover and simmer 30 minutes
- dice onion and sauté in a 10" frying pan with
  1 Tbls.oil - till very brown - about 10 minutes on medium
  - the browned onion makes for a meatier flavor
- remove tofu from packaging and pat with paper towels
- place in a large bowl and mash well with a fork
- tear bread into raisin size pieces and add to tofu
- add potato flakes <u>or</u> oats
- sprinkle all spices and 1/4 to 1/2 tsp.salt over
- add soup mix - and mix well
- drizzle 2 Tbls.oil over mixture
- add lightly beaten egg - mix again
- using a rubber spatula add the onion with all the rich pan drippings
- add the nuts
- drain lentils in strainer saving 1/2 cup liquid - throw
  away bay leaf - add lentils and liquid to tofu and mix well
- grease a 9x5 bread pan - we use 1 Tbls.butter here
- press the mixture in firmly with the back of a large spoon
- frost with 2 or more Tbls.ketchup - we like more
- bake 350° uncovered 45 minutes
- slice in 1/2 inch thick pieces.

Pot roast dinner

An old-fashioned and complete meal.
Serves: 2 - 3
Prep time: 20 minutes + 20 minutes defrost - refer to p.2
Cooking time: 2 hours

Ingredients:
- one pound **regular tofu - frozen and thawed**
- fat - we use canola oil and some butter here - but
  any vegetable oil and margarine will do
- 2 tsp.onion powder - not onion salt
- 1/2 tsp.garlic powder - not garlic salt
- 1/4 to 1/2 tsp.salt - use sea salt if you have it
- 1/8 tsp.pepper - we prefer fresh cracked
- 1 package dry onion-mushroom <u>or</u> beefy-onion soup mix
- 1 Tbls.soy sauce
- 2 large russet baking potatoes - we prefer Idaho
- 3 carrots
- *optional - 6 small or 3 large mushrooms*
- *optional - 9 cherry tomatoes or one big tomato*
- *optional - one medium size zucchini*
- 1 large yellow onion

How to:
- squeeze thawed tofu well - refer to thaw p.2
- slice into 5 equal slabs
- pour 3 Tbls.oil into a deep 12" fry pan or Dutch oven
- lay in tofu - sprinkle evenly with all spices and soup mix
  and pat down with a fork to mash lumps
- mix soy sauce into 1 cup water - we prefer filtered
- pour over tofu - bring to boil - cover tightly and turn
  down to simmer - 1 hour and 15 minutes
- scrub all veggies - leave skins on
- slice potatoes and carrots into 1/2 inch rounds
- *cut large mushrooms in-half - leave small ones whole*
- *leave cherry tomatoes whole - cut big tomato into 4 wedges*
- *slice zucchini into 1" rounds*
- peel onion and cut into 8 wedges
- arrange veggies in with pot roast - bring to a boil - turn
  down to low - cover and simmer 30 minutes - till
  potatoes are tender
- before serving - add a few pats of butter on top to melt.

Italian

Parmesan cutlets

A quick light meal. Try serving with hot buttered Italian bread - a toss green salad and balsamic vinegar dressing. These cutlets also make a great cold sandwich with lettuce and thick slices of tomato.
Serves: 2 - 3
Prep time: 10 minutes
Cooking time: 15 minutes

Ingredients:
- one pound **firm tofu - fresh**
- 1 cup grated parmesan cheese
- 1/2 tsp.garlic powder - not garlic salt
- 2 tsp.onion powder - not onion salt
- 1/8 tsp.pepper
- 3 Tbls.oil - we only use olive here - canola is okay
- 12 oz.can or jar of spaghetti or Alfredo sauce - or
  if you're ambitious make the sauce on p.34

How to:
- slice tofu into 5 equal slabs - and cut those across
  to make 10 squares
- mix 3/4 cup parmesan and all spices in a soup bowl
- pour 2 Tbls.oil into a 12" frying pan and turn
  burner to medium
- coat cutlets on all sides - pressing lightly to make
  as much of the mixture stick as possible
- lay into hot oil and brown - about 5 minutes
- add 1 Tbls.oil to pan
- turn cutlets over carefully so as not to break them
- sprinkle the rest of the parmesan mixture evenly over
  and brown 5 minutes more
- meanwhile heat the sauce - microwave or stove top
- serve cutlets on a heated platter with sauce spooned over
  and sprinkled with the remaining parmesan.

Pasta in spinach sauce

This is one of our favorites.
Serves: 2 - 3 - this recipe easily doubles for 5 or 6
Prep time: 20 minutes + 10 minutes defrost
Cooking time: 15 minutes

Ingredients:
- 1/2 pound **regular tofu - fresh**
- 1 cup ricotta cheese
- 1/4 cup milk or cream
- 1/2 tsp.ground nutmeg
- 1/2 to 3/4 tsp.salt
- 1/8 tsp.pepper - we like white pepper here
- 1/2 cup butter <u>or</u> margarine - we only use margarine that's
  non-hydrogenated and free of trans-fatty acids
- two 12 oz.packages chopped frozen spinach - completely
  thawed and squeezed - we thaw in the microwave - and
  squeeze using a strainer and the back of a big spoon
- enough dry fettuccini for 2 or 3 people
- 1/2 cup grated parmesan cheese for cooking
- extra parmesan for the table

How to:
- in a bowl - mash tofu to the texture of large curd
  cottage cheese
- add ricotta - milk and spices - and mix
- in a deep 12" fry pan - melt butter - add spinach and
  tofu-ricotta - mix - cover and heat on medium-low
  for 10 minutes - <u>do not let this mixture boil</u>
- stir in 1/2 cup parmesan cheese
- while that's heating - cook pasta according to package
  - drain well - transfer to a heated platter - we
  heat the platter by running hot water over both sides
  for a total of 10 seconds
- pour sauce over pasta
- and place the extra parmesan on the table.

Olive mushroom pizza pie

When it's gota be pizza - this will do it.
Serves: 2 - 3
Prep time: 45 minutes + 20 minutes defrost - refer to p.2
Baking time: 10 minutes

Ingredients:
- one pound **regular tofu - frozen and thawed**
- oil - we only use olive here - canola is okay
- 1 Tbls.onion powder - not onion salt
- 1/2 tsp.garlic powder - not garlic salt
- 1/4 to 1/2 tsp.salt
- 1/4 tsp.pepper - fresh cracked
- 1 cube vegetable or beef bouillon or 1 tsp.granules - we like Knorr
  - but any brand is fine
- 1 pound fresh mushrooms or one 4 oz.can sliced
- 1 unsliced loaf fresh Italian or French bread
- one 12 oz.jar or can of pizza or spaghetti sauce - or
  if you're feeling ambitious make the sauce on p.34
- one 4 oz.can sliced black olives - well drained
- 1/3 cup grated parmesan cheese
- 1 pound grated mozzarella cheese

How to:
- squeeze thawed tofu well - refer to thaw p.2
- now cut 8 equal slices - then chop or tear
  those into 1/2 inch pieces
- pour 2 Tbls.oil into a 12" frying pan - heat on medium
- add tofu to pan - sprinkle evenly with spices
- dissolve bouillon in 1/3 cup boiling water
- pour into pan and stir-fry uncovered till tofu is
  browned and all the liquid is gone - about
  10 minutes - put tofu aside in a bowl
- add 1 Tbls.oil to same fry pan
- slice mushrooms and sauté 5 minutes - if using
  canned - drain well and go to the next step
- add mushrooms - and 1 Tbls.oil if using canned - to tofu
- cut the ends off bread - then cut 6 thick slices
- turn oven on to broil
- lay slices on a cookie sheet - brush with olive
  oil and place under the broiler - keeping
  a watch till well browned - about 3 minutes
- turn slices over and spread liberally with sauce
- mix olives with mushrooms and tofu - divide
  evenly among the slices - spread over sauce
- sprinkle with parmesan
- finish with mozzarella
- place under broiler again and toast till the edges
  and cheese are well browned - about 5 minutes.

Pasta with savory sauce

We serve this mouth-watering dish at room temperature
instead of piping hot.
Serves: 2 - 3
Prep time: 25 minutes
Cooking time: 35 minutes

Ingredients:
- one pound **firm tofu - fresh**
- oil - we only use olive here - canola is okay
- 2 large cloves garlic chopped fine - <u>or</u> 1/2
  tsp.garlic powder - not garlic salt
- 1/2 pound fresh mushrooms sliced <u>or</u> one 4 oz.can sliced
  and well drained
- 1 bunch scallions cut into 1 inch pieces
- 1 medium size zucchini sliced into 1/4 inch rounds
- 1 beef or vegetable bouillon cube <u>or</u> 1 tsp.granules - we use Knorr
  - but any brand is fine
- 1/4 to 1/2 tsp.salt
- 3 large tomatoes each cut into 8 wedges - <u>or</u>
  one 14 oz.can tomatoes diced
- fresh finely chopped basil <u>or</u> 1/2 tsp.dry rosemary crushed
- enough pasta for 2 or 3 people - we use Rotini but
  fettuccini or medium size shells will do
- 1/4 cup parmesan cheese

 How to:
- pour 2 Tbls.oil in a deep 12" fry pan and place
  on medium heat
- add garlic
- cut tofu into 6 equal slabs - cut each slab across into
  8 equal sticks - and cut those in half - add to garlic and
  stir-fry gently using a wooden spoon so as not to break
  up the tofu - about 5 minutes
- add mushrooms to pan - stir-fry 5 minutes
- add scallions and zucchini - stir-fry 5 minutes
- mix bouillon into 3/4 cup boiling water and add
- sprinkle with salt
- simmer uncovered - stirring once or twice - till
  most of the liquid is gone - about 10 minutes
- cook pasta according to package directions
- add tomatoes and 1/4 cup basil <u>or</u> 1/2 tsp.dry rosemary to tofu
  and simmer - 10 minutes
- serve pasta on a platter with sauce poured over
- garnish with parmesan cheese and more fresh chopped basil if
  you have it.

Baked Italian wraps

So good you'll make them often.
Serves: 4
Prep time: 25 minutes
Baking time: 45 minutes

Ingredients:
- one pound **regular to firm tofu - fresh**
- 2 Tbls.oil - we only use olive here - canola is okay
- 1/2 pound fresh mushrooms <u>or</u> one 4 oz.can - well drained
- 2 large cloves garlic <u>or</u> 3/4 tsp.garlic powder
- 1 bunch scallions
- 1 tsp.dry crushed rosemary <u>or</u> 1/4 cup fresh chopped basil
- 2 tsp.dry soup granules or 2 bouillon cubes - beef - vegetable
  <u>or</u> chicken - dissolved in 1 cup boiling water - we use
  Knorr but any brand is fine
- one 16 oz.can or jar spaghetti sauce - <u>or</u> if
  you're feeling ambitious - make the sauce on p.34
- 6 giant flour tortillas - you could also use tomato or spinach wraps
- 1 cup grated parmesan cheese

How to:
- slice tofu into 6 equal slabs
- pour 1 Tbls.oil in deep 12" fry pan - turn burner to medium
- add tofu - sprinkle with garlic powder here if
  you're not using fresh chopped
- chop mushrooms - garlic and onions - and spread over tofu
- add rosemary <u>or</u> basil
- pour bouillon over and bring to a boil - turn down
  and simmer till all liquid is gone - about 10 minutes
- turn oven to 325°
- pour 1 Tbls.oil and 1 cup sauce into a 9x12x3 baking dish
- now lay a tortilla on a large plate and place one
  tofu cutlet in the center
- add 1/6th of the mushroom mixture
- and 1 heaping Tbls.parmesan
- fold bottom of tortilla up over filling - fold sides in -
  - roll over top - and place seam side down into baking dish
- repeat for the rest of the tortillas
- pour sauce over all - sprinkle with the remaining parmesan
- cover with tin foil and bake 45 minutes
- if you want - you can turn the oven off after baking and
  leave the wraps for up to 1 hour before serving - without
  needing to re-heat.

Lasagna

This dish is well worth the time and effort - and convenient made-up the day before and cooked the day of.
Serves: 4
Prep time: 30 minutes
Baking time: 60 minutes

Ingredients:
- one pound **regular tofu - fresh**
- 2 Tbls.oil - we only use olive here - canola is okay
- 1 pound mushrooms sliced thin - or one 8 oz.can sliced
  and well drained
- 1 package dry soup mix - onion-mushroom or savory
  herb with garlic or beefy-onion - mixed into 1 cup boiled water
- 1 heaping tsp.crushed rosemary
- one package lasagna noodles
- one 26 oz.can or jar spaghetti sauce - your choice - or
  if you're feeling ambitious make the sauce on p.34
- 1 cup grated parmesan or Romano cheese
- 2 lbs.mozzarella cheese - sliced thin

How to:
- if using fresh mushrooms - pour oil into a 10" frying
  pan - add mushrooms - sauté 10 minutes – then add soup mix
  and rosemary - bring to a boil and remove from burner
- if using canned mushrooms - combine in a sauce pot with oil – soup
  mix and rosemary - bring to a boil - and remove from burner
- cook noodles according to package
- while noodles are draining - turn oven to 325°
- now pour one cup spaghetti sauce into a 9x13 baking dish
- lay in 1/2 of the noodles to cover bottom
- slice tofu into 9 equal slabs and lay over noodles
- sprinkle with 1/3 cup parmesan
- pour mushroom mixture over
- cover with 1/2 the remaining spaghetti sauce
- arrange 1/2 of the sliced mozzarella cheese over sauce
- lay the rest of the noodles over mozzarella
- sprinkle with 1/3 cup parmesan
- lay the remaining mozzarella over
- cover with the rest of the sauce
- sprinkle with 1/3 cup parmesan
- cover with tin foil and bake - 1 hour
- we like to let this dish cool on the counter 30 minutes
  before serving.

Eggplant pasta feast

You can make this the day before and store covered in the refrigerator. It's the perfect autumn dinner party meal served with a green salad, vinegar and oil dressing, and hot Italian bread.

Serves: 6
Prep time: 60 minutes
Baking time: 60 minutes
Ingredients:
- two pounds **regular tofu - fresh**
- oil - we only use olive here - canola is okay
- 1 package dry soup mix - savory herb-garlic <u>or</u> beefy-onion
- 1 large yellow onion
- 2 large cloves garlic
- 1 pound mushrooms <u>or</u> one 8 oz.can - well drained
- one large eggplant
- 1 large zucchini
- 14 oz.dry pasta - small shells <u>or</u> ziti <u>or</u> mustacholli
- one 16 oz.can or jar of spaghetti sauce - <u>or</u> if
  you're feeling ambitious make the sauce on p.34
- basil - 1/2 cup fresh chopped <u>or</u> 1 heaping tsp.dry crushed
- 1 cup grated parmesan cheese
- 1 pint ricotta cheese

How to:
- cut each pound of tofu into 6 slabs - cut those in half
  and cut again into thirds
- pour 2 Tbls.oil into a deep 12" fry pan or Dutch oven
- add tofu - sprinkle dry soup over and turn burner to medium
- slice onion - garlic and mushrooms thin and lay over tofu
- pour in 1 cup water - bring to boil - turn down to
  low - cover and simmer for 30 minutes
- now turn oven to 325°
- slice eggplant and zucchini into 1/2 inch rounds
- place on cookie sheet - brush liberally with oil
- bake 30 minutes - eggplant should be completely soft
- now cook pasta according to package directions - drain
- pour 2 Tbls.oil into a 9x14x3 glass baking dish - add 1/3 of the sauce
- sprinkle basil over sauce - add pasta and mix till coated
- spread evenly in pan and sprinkle with 1/4 cup parmesan
- dot with ricotta
- lay zucchini over - then eggplant
- drizzle 1/3 sauce evenly over
- spoon on the tofu mixture - then pour pan juice over
- sprinkle with 3/4 cup parmesan
- pour the rest of the sauce evenly over
- cover with tin foil - turn oven to 350° and bake 50 minutes
- remove tin foil the last 10 minutes
- before serving - sprinkle with more parmesan - and if
  you used the fresh chopped basil - sprinkle on another 1/4 cup.

Superb spaghetti sauce

We make our sauce in a crock pot and never have to tend it. If you don't have one - bake it in the oven - just make sure the handles on your pot and lid are oven safe. Use this sauce on pasta - when making lasagna or pizza - or our favorite - over polenta.

Serves: 4 to 6
Prep time: 10 minutes + 20 minutes defrost - refer to p.2
Cooking time: crock pot on low - 8 hours — on high - 4 hours — or baked in the oven at 300° for 3 hours

Ingredients:
- one pound **regular tofu - frozen and thawed**
- 3 Tbls.oil - we only use olive here - canola is okay
- one 12 oz.can tomato paste
- 2 vegetable or beef bouillon cubes or 1 Tbls.granules dissolved in
  16 oz.boiling water - we like Knorr but any brand is fine
- one 12 oz.can diced tomatoes in natural juice
- 1 pound fresh mushrooms - we pick out the smallest ones
  and leave them whole - or use one 8 oz.can of whole
- 1 bunch scallions - sliced very fine
- 3 cloves finely minced garlic
- 1/2 tsp.cinnamon
- a pinch of cayenne
- 1 tsp.dry crushed rosemary
- 1 tsp.dry crushed basil
- 1 tsp.dry crushed oregano
- 1 tsp.sugar
- 1/2 to 1 tsp.salt - we prefer sea salt

How to:
- pour oil into pot
- add broth and tomato paste and stir with a whisk
  till smooth
- squeeze thawed tofu - refer to thaw - p.2
- cut into 8 equal slabs - tear each into raisin
  size pieces and add to pot
- add tomatoes
- add the rest of the ingredients in order - mix well
- if using crock pot on low - cover and simmer - 8 hours
- if using crock pot on high - cover and simmer - 4 hours
- if using oven - cover and bake at 300° - 3 hours.

Asian

Instant Asian nuggets

Prepare these tasty morsels - then pick any packaged Asian seasoning mix and follow the directions using them instead of meat.
Serves: 2 - 3
Prep time: 10 minutes
Cooking time: 20 minutes

Ingredients:
- one pound **firm tofu - fresh**
- 1 1/2 Tbls.oil - we use canola or corn here
- 1 tsp.onion powder - not onion salt
- 1 heaping tsp.soup granules - what ever flavor
  the seasoning mix calls for - dissolved in 1/4 cup
  boiling water - we like Knorr but any brand is fine
- 1/4 cup soy sauce - we prefer tamari

How to:
- cut tofu into 6 equal slabs - then into 1" cubes
- place oil in a 10" frying pan - heat on medium
- lay in tofu
- sprinkle with onion powder
- fry till golden brown on all sides - about 10 minutes
- pour soup and soy sauce over
- continue cooking uncovered till all the liquid is gone -
  about 10 minutes
- now - follow the seasoning mix directions and use these
  nuggets as you would meat.

Kim chee over rice

No matter who we serve this dish to - they rave over it.
Serves: 2 - 3
Prep time: 20 minutes
Cooking time: 20 minutes

Ingredients:
- one pound **regular tofu - fresh**
- rice - you may want to look at p.44
- 1 1/2 Tbls.oil - we like olive or canola here
- 3 large cloves garlic
- 2 bunches scallions
- one large nappa cabbage
- 1 cube vegetable bouillon dissolved in 1/4 cup boiling
  water - we use Knorr here but any brand is fine
- 2 Tbls.soy sauce - we prefer tamari
- 1/4 to 1/2 tsp.fresh ground chili paste
- 1 1/2 Tbls.corn starch - mixed into 1/2 cup <u>cold</u> water
- 2 ripe oranges

How to:
- put rice on to cook according to directions
- pour oil into a deep 12" fry pan and heat on medium
- chop garlic fine and add to oil
- slice tofu into 6 equal slabs - cut those into 1" cubes
- add tofu to garlic and stir-fry with a wooden spoon
  - being careful not to break-up the tofu - about 5 minute
- slice scallions into 1" pieces - add to pan - do <u>not</u> mix
- starting at the leaf tips - cut nappa cabbage across into
  1/4" slices - throwing away the bottom 2 inches of stem
- add to pan - do <u>not</u> mix
- add soy sauce and chili paste to bouillon - pour
  into pan - cover immediately and steam till cabbage
  is soft - about 8 minutes
- gently mix cabbage and onions into tofu
- now - stir-up corn starch and water and pour evenly over
- mixing gently - bring to a boil - and as soon as the
  sauce has thickened - cover and remove from heat
- serve rice on a warmed platter with kim chee and all
  the sauce spooned over - trim the edges with thin
  sliced oranges - and put the bottle of soy sauce on
  the table.

Sesame cutlets with plum sauce over rice

Simple - quick - fabulous.
Serves: 2 - 3
Prep time: 20 minutes
Cooking time: 25 minutes

Ingredients:
- one pound **firm tofu - fresh**
- quick rice for 2 or 3 - <u>or</u> you may want to check out p.44
- 2 to 3 cups frozen vegetables - we use a packaged medley
  of red bell peppers - broccoli - mushrooms and pea pods
- 2 Tbls.corn starch
- 1 Tbls.white flour - we like Wondera here
- 1/4 to 1/2 tsp.salt
- 1 tsp.onion powder - not onion salt
- 1 tsp.ground ginger
- 2 egg whites
- 1/2 cup raw white sesame seeds
- 3 Tbls.oil - we use canola here - but any vegetable is okay
- 1 bunch scallions - chopped
- 6 oz.plum jelly
- 3 Tbls.vinegar - we prefer rice vinegar here
- 1/4 cup soy sauce

How to:
- put rice on to cook according to directions
- put veggies on to cook - we steam ours
- slice tofu into 6 equal slabs - cut those across one time
- lay tofu on paper towels - turning over once to dry
- using a whisk - mix corn starch - flour - salt -
  onion powder and ginger in a soup bowl
- beat egg whites till foamy in another soup bowl
- and place sesame seeds in a third soup bowl
- pour 2 Tbls.oil in a deep 12" fry pan and turn burner to medium
- add chopped scallions to oil
- dip each cutlet in flour mixture - covering all sides
- dip in egg whites
- now dredge in sesame seeds - coating cutlets well
  on all sides
- lay them in the hot oil and fry till sesame seeds are brown
- add 1 Tbls.oil - turn over only once and brown
- in a small sauce pan - mix jelly - vinegar - soy sauce
  - and heat till jelly is melted - do <u>not</u> boil
- serve vegetables and cutlets over rice on a warmed
  platter with plum sauce drizzled over all.

Saucy sweet and sour supper

This is quick and light and we serve it on couscous - but it's just as yummy over rice.
You can use fresh or frozen vegetables.
Serves: 2 - 3
Prep time: 30 minutes
Cooking time: 25 minutes

Ingredients:
- one pound **regular to firm tofu - fresh**
- couscous or quick rice for 2 or 3
- 2 Tlbs.oil - we use corn here but any vegetable is okay
- 1/4 cup soy sauce - we like tamari
- 2 1/2 Tbls.brown sugar
- 3 Tbls.vinegar - apple cider is best here
- 3/4 tsp.garlic powder - not garlic salt
- 1/2 tsp.onion powder - not onion salt
- 1/4 tsp.dry mustard
- 1/2 tsp.ground ginger
- 1 Tbls.corn starch dissolved in 2 Tbls.cold water
- 1 cup broccoli – chopped – fresh or frozen
- 2 carrots – chopped – fresh or frozen
- 1 red or green pepper – chopped – fresh or frozen
- 1 bunch scallions – chopped – fresh or frozen

How to:
- cut tofu into 6 equal slabs - then into 1" cubes
- put couscous or rice on to cook following package directions
- for rice check-out p.44
- pour oil into a deep 12" frying pan
- add tofu and sauté on medium till golden brown on at least two sides -
  use a wooden spoon so as not to break-up the cubes
- while that's browning - whisk together in a small sauce pan on medium-low heat -
  1/2 cup water - soy sauce - sugar - vinegar - garlic and onion powders -
  mustard and ginger - bring only to a simmer - do not boil
- stir-up corn starch/water mixture and whisk into sauce
- cook only till thickened and smooth - about 1 minute or less
  - then remove from burner
- add broccoli - carrots - bell pepper and scallions to tofu and stir-fry - 10 minutes
- add sauce - cover - simmer 2 minutes
- serve on a warmed platter over couscous or rice.

Richard's favorite tofu

You will think people who make fun of tofu are nuts once you've tried this recipe. We serve it over rice and steamed broccoli - garnished with chopped fresh cilantro. It's also delicious hot or cold on a sandwich - just make sure the bread is fresh - we prefer whole wheat - lots of mayo - a smear of hot sweet mustard - and some red leaf lettuce.

Serves: 2 - 3
Prep time: 10 minutes + 20 minutes defrost - refer to p.2
Cooking time: 50 minutes

Ingredients:
- one pound **regular tofu - frozen and thawed**
- 1 1/2 Tbls.oil - we use canola here - but any oil is okay
- 1/2 tsp.garlic powder - not garlic salt
- 1 tsp.onion powder - not onion salt
- 1/2 tsp.ground ginger
- 1/8 to 1/4 tsp.cayenne pepper
- 1/4 tsp.black pepper - we prefer fresh cracked
- 2 tsp.toasted sesame seeds - you can toast you own
  by placing the seeds in a dry fry pan over medium heat
  and stirring constantly till brown - about 5 minutes
- 1/4 cup honey - use 1/3 cup if you like it sweeter
- 3 Tbls.soy sauce - we prefer tamari
- 1 bouillon cube <u>or</u> 1 tsp.soup granules – beef - chicken
  or vegetable - dissolved in 3/4 cup boiling water - we use
  Knorr but you can use any brand

How to:
- squeeze thawed tofu well - refer to thaw p.2
- slice into 6 equal cutlets
- pour oil in a 10" frying pan
- lay in cutlets
- evenly sprinkle on spices and sesame seeds
- drizzle honey liberally over each cutlet
- pour in soy sauce and bouillon
- bring to a boil - turn down - cover and simmer - 1 hour
  - turning cutlets over once after 30 minutes
* if you're serving this dish hot - pour sauce over rice -
  you may want to use the Perfect rice recipe on p.44
* if you are going for sandwiches - drain cutlets using
  a slotted spatula - and if there is any left over - store cutlets separate
  from sauce - you can use the sauce to flavor tomorrow's rice or noodles.

Curried bean curds and yams

A wonderfully fragrant and satisfying one pan meal. On a late Autumn day when the yams are fresh - just put this on to simmer and forget it. Best served over basmati-jasmine rice.
Serves: 2 - 3
Prep time: 15 minutes
Cooking time: 1 hour

Ingredients:
- one pound **regular tofu - fresh**
- 3 Tbls.fat - butter <u>or</u> margarine - we only use margarine
  that is no-hydrogenated and has no trans-fatty acids
- 1 large yellow onion - sliced thin
- 1 tart apple sliced thin - we use a granny smith
- 2 large cloves garlic - minced
- 2 medium-large yams
- one 16 oz.can peach halves in heavy syrup
- 1 Tbls.soup granules - vegetable or chicken - we like
  Knorr but you can use any brand
- 1 tsp.curry powder
- 1/4 cup honey
- quick rice for 2 or 3 - or you may want to check out p.44
- 1/3 cup cold evaporated milk
- 1 heaping Tbls.corn starch

How to:
- put fat into a deep 12" fry pan and turn burner to medium
- sauté onion and apple - about 5 minutes
- add garlic and sauté 2 minutes
- slice tofu into 6 equal slabs - cut into 1" cubes
- add to pan and sauté 5 minutes
- skin yams - slice into 1/2 inch rounds and lay over tofu
- pour peach juice into a measuring cup - add enough water
  to make 1 cup - now heat this in a small sauce pan
- when hot but not boiling remove from burner and
  dissolve soup and curry powder in it
- lay peaches around potatoes
- pour curry/soup over
- drizzle honey on evenly
- cover and simmer 45 minutes - till potatoes are soft
- make rice according to directions
- just before serving - mix corn starch into evaporated
  milk - pour evenly over curry - stirring very gently
  just till sauce has thickened
- cover - take off burner and let sit 5 minutes
- serve curry along side rice - not spooned over.

Stuffed nappa cabbage

This is mom's stuffed cabbage recipe gone Asian. We serve steamed broccoli and extra rice with it - a mix of canned lychee nuts and mandarin oranges - and warmed sake.
Serves: 4 - 5
Prep time: 35 minutes
Baking time: 45 minutes

Ingredients:
- one pound **regular tofu - fresh**
- 1 1/2 cups dry rice - we use white basmati and jasmine
  - look at p.44 for Perfect rice every time
- 3 tsp.soup granules - beef <u>or</u> vegetable - we like Knorr
  but you can use any brand
- 2 Tbls.oil - we prefer canola or olive here
- 2 bunches scallions - chopped fine
- 1 tsp.salt
- 1 large nappa cabbage
- 1 tsp.onion powder - not onion salt
- 1/4 tsp.black pepper
- 1/3 cup raisins - we like white raisins but dark will do
- 1 Tbls.fat - butter <u>or</u> margarine - we only use margarine
  that is non-hydrogenated and had no trans-fatty acids
- one crisp apple - we prefer a fuji
- 8 oz.grape jelly
- 1/4 cup vinegar - we like rice or apple cider here
- 1/2 cup apple juice

How to:
- put rice on to cook according to package directions
  - substituting 1 tsp.soup granules for salt
- in a 10" fry pan - sauté scallions in 2 Tbls.oil - 5 minutes on medium
- place the largest cabbage leaves in a pot of boiling water with salt for one
  minute – plunge immediately into cold water – then drain in a strainer
- mash tofu in large bowl with a fork or pastry blender
- add cooked rice - scallions and oil from pan
- mix thoroughly with a spoon
- add onion powder - pepper - 1 tsp.soup granules - and raisins - mix well
- grease a 9x13 glass baking pan with fat
- core apple - slice very thin and lay over bottom of pan
- place equal amounts of filling in the center of each
  cabbage leaf - fold the thick end over filling - the sides in - and roll up
- set cabbage rolls seam side down close together on apples
- now - in a small sauce pan - using a whisk - melt jelly
  with vinegar and juice - do <u>not</u> boil
- add 1 tsp.soup granules - cook stirring constantly
  till granules are completely dissolved - do <u>not</u> boil
- pour sauce over cabbage
- bake 350° - 45 minutes - basting often with sauce.

Perfect rice every time

First of all - you must start with good rice. We always use a 50-50 mix of aged white basmati and jasmine rice. Buy both and mix them together in a large container.

You need a good quality oil. We prefer extra virgin olive no matter what type of cooking we're doing.

We always use sea salt - and filtered water.

This step is crucial - before cooking - rinse the rice in a fine wire mesh strainer for 15 seconds under cold water - let drain 5 minutes - and repeat.

And - you absolutely must use a thick bottomed 3 quart stainless steel pot with a tight fitting lid.

Serves: 2-3 - this recipe doubles easily
Prep time: 5 minutes
Cooking time: 25 minutes

Ingredients:
- 1 cup dry rice
- 2 cups water
- 1 Tbls.oil
- 1/2 tsp.salt

How to:
- measure rice into strainer - rinse and drain twice
- pour water - oil and salt into pot and bring to an active boil
- dump in rice and stir only once to mix
- let the pot come back to boil - turn burner down to the lowest setting - wait till boiling calms - cover - spin the lid to create a good seal - and do not remove it for any reason till serving time
- set timer for 20 minutes
- when time is up - take rice pot off burner - you can serve it immediately - or leave it covered for up to half an hour - just remember - do not remove the lid till serving.

Mexican

The fastest meal in the West

Don't wana cook - don't wana go out - want something good.
Serves: 2 - 3
Prep time: 10 minutes
Cooking time: 10 minutes

Ingredients:
- one pound **regular tofu - fresh**
- instant rice for 2 or 3 people
- 1 Tbls.oil - we use corn here but any vegetable is okay
- 1 tsp.onion powder - not onion salt
- 1 package taco seasoning - we like McCormick's but any
  brand will do
- 1 cube vegetable or beef bouillon <u>or</u> 1 tsp.granules dissolved in 3/4
  cup boiling water - we prefer Knorr but any brand is fine
- 2 cups frozen vegetables - we use brocolli here
  but corn or green beans are just as good
- one 14 oz.can diced tomatoes - drained
- 1 cup grated cheddar or jack cheese
- your favorite bottled hot sauce or salsa

How to:
- put rice on to cook - according to package directions
- slice tofu into 6 equal slabs - then cut into 1" cubes
- pour oil into a deep 12" fry pan - turn burner to medium
- add tofu
- sprinkle evenly with onion powder and taco seasoning
- pour in bouillon
- place vegetables in between tofu
- pour on tomatoes
- bring to a boil - turn down - cover and simmer 10 minutes
- serve over rice
- sprinkle liberally with cheese
- and put the hot sauce and salsa on the table.

Instant homemade chili

Open the cans - simmer ten minutes – dinner. We like our chili with shredded cheddar and fresh chopped cilantro on top - corn chips and salsa on the side.
Serves: 3 - 4
Prep time: 15 minutes
Cooking time: 15 minutes

Ingredients:
- one pound **firm tofu - fresh**
- 2 Tbls.oil - we only use corn here - canola will do
- one 15 oz.can cooked pinto beans
- one 14 oz.can diced tomatoes
- one 8 oz.can tomato sauce
- *optional - one 8 oz.can corn - drained*
- 1 cube <u>or</u> 1 tsp.bouillon - beef - vegetable or chicken - dissolved
  in 1/4 cup boiling water - we use Knorr - use your favorite brand
- 1 package chili seasoning mix - we like McCormick's but
  any brand is fine
- 1 Tbls.corn meal stirred into 1/2 cup <u>cold</u> water
- your favorite corn chips
- 2 cups shredded cheddar
- *optional - 1 cup fresh cilantro - chopped*
- bottled salsa - or if you're feeling ambitious - try p.54

How to:
- slice tofu into 8 slabs - and cut into 1/2" cubes
- pour oil into a large heavy-bottomed pot and turn
  burner to medium
- add tofu
- pour in pinto beans and liquid from can
- add tomatoes - and tomato sauce
- *and corn*
- add bouillon and chili seasoning
- mix - using a wooden spoon so as not to break up the tofu cubes
- bring to a boil - turn down - cover and simmer - 10 minutes
- stir-up corn meal mixture – add to pot - gently stirring to distribute
  - cover and cook 5 minutes
- just before serving - put chips in a large bowl and heat
  45 seconds in the microwave
- ladle chili into soup bowls - cover with cheese and *cilantro*
- and pass around the hot sauce and salsa.

Fajita heaven

After making this recipe - you may be disappointed the next time you go out for Mexican. Serve with corn chips and cold beer.

Serves: 3 - 4
Prep time: 20 minutes
Cooking time: 20 minutes

Ingredients:
- one pound **regular tofu - fresh**
- rice for 4 people - quick rice or use the recipe on p.44
- 2 Tbls.oil - we like corn here - canola is okay
- 1 large yellow onion
- 1 medium zucchini
- 8 medium size mushrooms or one well drained 4 oz.can sliced
- 1/2 tsp.garlic powder - not garlic salt
- 1 package fajita seasoning - we use McCormick's but any brand will do
- 1 cube or 1 tsp.vegetable or beef bouillon dissolved in 1/2 cup boiled water - we prefer Knorr - but any brand is fine
- one 8 oz.can tomato sauce
- one 14 oz.can diced tomatoes
- *optional - 2 cups grated cheddar or jack cheese*
- your favorite bag of corn chips
- bottled salsa - or if you're feeling ambitious - try the recipe on p.54

How to:
- put rice on to cook according to directions
- pour oil into a deep 12" fry pan and turn burner to medium
- cut tofu into 7 equal slabs - cut those into 1" cubes and add to oil
- slice onion - zucchini and mushrooms thin and lay over tofu
- sprinkle garlic and fajita seasoning on evenly
- pour bouillon over
- and tomato sauce
- and tomatoes
- bring to a boil - turn down - cover - simmer 20 minutes
- serve on a warmed platter over rice
- *sprinkled liberally with cheese*
- put corn chips in a bowl and heat 45 seconds in the microwave just before serving
- and pass the salsa round the table.

Savory burritos and rice

These burritos are real winners. We like ours with hot buttered cornbread on the side.
Serves: 3 - 4
Prep time: 25 minutes + 20 minutes defrost - refer to p.2
Cooking time: 35 minutes

Ingredients:
- one pound **regular tofu - frozen and thawed**
- 1 1/2 Tbls.oil - we only use corn here - canola is okay
- 1 tsp.onion powder - not onion salt
- 1 package burrito seasoning mix - we like McCormick's
  but any brand is fine
- 2 cups frozen chopped broccoli
- one 14 oz.can diced tomatoes
- 1 cube beef or vegetable bouillon <u>or</u> 1 tsp.granules dissolved in one
  cup boiling water - we like Knorr - but any brand will do
- quick rice for 4 <u>or</u> use the recipe on p.44
- 4 giant fresh flour tortilla shells
- *optional - 1 bunch fresh cilantro - chopped*
- 2 cups shredded cheddar or jack cheese
- your favorite hot sauce and salsa - if you're
  feeling ambitious - try the recipe on p.54

How to:
- squeeze thawed tofu well - refer to thaw p.2
- slice into 7 equal slabs - and cut into 1/2" cubes
- pour oil into a deep 12" fry pan - turn burner to medium
- add tofu
- sprinkle with onion powder and packaged seasoning mix
- add broccoli
- pour tomatoes and bouillon over all
- bring to a boil - turn down - cover and simmer - 30 minutes
- cook rice according to directions
- when everything is done - lay one tortilla on each plate
- place 1/2 cup rice in center
- using a slotted spoon - spoon 1/4th of the tofu mixture
over rice - leaving most of the sauce in the pan
- *add 1 Tbls.chopped cilantro*
- and 1/4 cup cheese
- bring tortilla bottom up over filling - fold in sides
  - roll up - and turn seam side down one to a plate
- divide remaining rice equally between plates
- spoon sauce from pan over all
- sprinkled with remaining cheese
- heat each plate in microwave till the cheese
  melts - about 1 minutes on medium
- place the hot sauce and salsa on the table.

♀

Tamale pie

This is a completely satisfying meal.
Serves: 3 - 4
Prep time: 45 minutes
Baking time: 90 minutes

Ingredients:
- one pound **regular tofu - fresh**
- 1 cup course ground yellow corn meal
- 1 cup milk
- salt
- fat - 2 Tbls.oil <u>and</u> 1 Tbls.butter or margarine
- 1 large yellow onion - chopped
- 1 green pepper - chopped
- 1 tsp.onion powder - not onion salt
- 1/2 tsp.garlic powder - not garlic salt
- 1/2 tsp.Mexican oregano - Italian is okay too
- 1 1/2 tsp.ground chili powder
- one 8 oz.can tomato sauce
- 1 cube vegetable or beef bouillon dissolved in 1/4 cup boiling water
- one 14 oz.can diced tomatoes - drained
- one 8 oz.can corn - drained
- one 3.5 oz.can sliced black olives - drained
- one 15 oz.can pinto beans - drained
- 2 eggs
- one 4 oz.can diced green chilies - drained
- 4 cups grated cheddar or jack cheese

How to:
- combine corn meal - milk and 3 1/2 cups water in a pot
- add 1/2 to 1 tsp.salt - and stirring often bring to a boil - turn
  down to simmer - 15 minutes - then take off burner to cool
- cut tofu into 1" cubes
- pour oil into a deep 12" fry pan - turn burner to medium
- add tofu - onion and green pepper - stir-fry - 10 minutes
- add 1/4 to 1/2 tsp.salt - onion and garlic powders - oregano
  - chili powder - 3/4 can tomato sauce - bouillon
  - turn burner down - cover and simmer - 10 minutes
- add tomatoes - corn - olives - beans - cover and simmer 5 minutes
- grease a 9x13 glass baking pan with 1 Tbls.butter
- spread 1 cup corn meal over bottom of pan
- add lightly beaten eggs to rest of corn meal and mix well
- add green chilies and 1 cup cheese - mix again
- spoon all the tofu filling over corn meal already in pan
- evenly sprinkle with 2 cups cheese
- cover with the corn meal and cheese mixture
- sprinkle on the rest of the cheese
- drizzle with remaining tomato sauce
- bake 1 1/2 hours - uncovered - 300°
- cool 20 minutes before serving.

♀

Longway chili

Everything you could want in a spicy thick chili. We serve it with fresh chopped cilantro and a dab of sour cream or mayo on top - and a thick slice of jalapeño cornbread on the side.
Serves: 4
Prep time: 20 minutes + 20 minutes defrost - refer to p.2
Cooking time: 2 hours 15 minutes

Ingredients:
- one pound **regular tofu - frozen and thawed**
- 2 cups dry pinto beans
- 3 Tbls.oil - we prefer corn here - canola is okay
- 1/4 to 1/2 tsp.salt
- 1 tsp.ground cumin
- 1/4 tsp.cayenne
- 1 package onion-mushroom or beefy-onion soup mix
- 1/2 tsp.garlic powder - not garlic salt
- 1 tsp.onion powder - not onion salt
- one 6 oz.can tomato paste
- one 14 oz.can diced tomatoes
- 3 Tbls.corn meal - mixed with 1/2 cup <u>cold</u> water

How to
- pick over and wash beans - put in a bowl - cover with
  water - soak overnight - 8-12 hours
- rinse beans and place in large soup pot - add 6 cups water
- bring to a boil - turn down - cover and simmer 1 hour -
  stirring every 15 minutes
- squeeze tofu well - slice into 7 equal slabs - and
  crumble into the bean pot by tearing each slab
  into small pieces
- add oil - salt - cumin - cayenne - soup mix - garlic
  and onion powders - tomato paste - tomatoes - mix well
- bring to a boil - turn down - cover - simmer 1 more hour
  - stirring every 15 minute
- the last 15 minutes - stir-in the corn meal and cold water.

The best beans

These are wonderful tender meaty beans - and easy to prepare. If you use a crock pot - they're ready when you come home. We like them over polenta with grated cheddar cheese - and the salsa on p.54. They store well in the frig – 4 days - and freeze beautifully. You can use them in burritos - tacos - fajitas - over mashed potatoes - rice - or pasta - or along side hot buttered cornbread and honey.

Serves: 6

Prep time: 15 minutes + 20 minutes defrost - refer to p.2

Cooking time: crock pot on low 10 hours - on high 4 hours — baked in the oven 4 hours — simmered atop the stove 2 hours

Ingredients:
- one pound **regular tofu - frozen and thawed**
- 2 cups dry pinto beans
- 1 cube bouillon - beef – tomato or vegetable - we use Knorr
  but any brand if fine
- 1 package onion-mushroom or beefy-onion soup mix
- 1 tsp.ground cumin
- 3 Tbls.oil - we use corn here but canola is okay
- 1 Tbls.soy sauce - we prefer tamari
- 1/4 cup cornmeal and 1/2 cup cold water

How to:
- before going to bed - pick over beans - wash - place
  in bowl - cover with 6 cups water and soak over night
- also - defrost the tofu - refer to thaw p.2 - and store
  it in the frig over night
- in the morning - rinse and drain beans and place in pot
- add 5 cups water - we like filtered
- squeeze thawed tofu - slice into 10 equal slabs -
  and cut those into raisin size pieces - add to beans
- add bouillon - soup mix - cumin - oil and soy sauce
- stir to mix
- if slow crock-potting - turn to low - cover and forget
  for 10 hours
- if fast crock-potting - turn to high - cover and cook
  3 - 4 hours - stirring once every hour
- if baking - bring to a boil atop of the stove
  - stir - cover and bake at 325° - 4 hours - and make
  sure your pot handles are oven proof
- if cooking atop of the stove - bring to a boil -
  turn burner down to low - cover and simmer 2 hours
  - stirring every half hour
- to thicken - mix cornmeal and cold water - and stir into
  beans 15 minutes before they're done.

Salsa supreme

We use this on everything. Think of it as salsa - or as a marinated salad served on chopped iceberg lettuce. It keeps one week in the frig - but never lasts that long.
Serves: 8 as salsa - 4 as salad
Prep time: 15 minutes + 1 hour chill time
Cooking time: 5 minutes

Ingredients:
- 2 fresh ears yellow or white corn - <u>or</u> if you have to - one
  11 oz.can tender young sweet corn - well drained
- one 14 oz.can diced peeled tomatoes - drained
- one 4 oz.can chopped green chilies - drained
- 1/2 sweet Vidalia - Bermuda or Walla Walla onion - it
  must be a mild sweet onion - taste before using and if
  it has any bite - leave it out
- 1 cup fresh cilantro leaves
- *optional - green pickled jalapeño peppers*
- 6 oz.bottle of green taco sauce
- 1 Tbls.vinegar - we prefer apple cider
- 1 Tbls.fresh squeezed lime juice - fresh is a must
- 1/2 to 1 tsp.salt - we use sea salt for all the good minerals
- 1 tsp.sugar
- 1 1/2 Tbls.oil - we prefer corn here
- 1-2 tsp.hot sauce - depending on how much zing you
  like in your salsa - we use Trappey's mexi-pep but any
  brand is fine
- 1/4 tsp.ground cumin
- 1/4 tsp.coriander

How to:
- if using fresh corn - husk - wash well - place both ears
  in the same plastic bag - microwave on high 3 minutes
  - turn corn over - microwave 3 more minutes
- using a small knife - cut corn off cob into a 3 quart mixing bowl
- combine tomatoes and chilies with corn
- chop onion fine and add
- chop cilantro and add 1/2 cup
- *chop jalapeños and add - we use about 1 tsp.but you can add
  more or less - or none depending on your taste buds*
- in 1 quart bowl - combine taco sauce - vinegar - lime juice
  - salt - sugar - oil - hot sauce - cumin and coriander
- beat with a whisk
- pour over salsa and mix well
- taste - you may want to add more salt - or hot sauce
  - or jalapeños - or even maybe 1/2 tsp.more sugar
- cover and chill at least 1 hour.

Soups and stews

Chicken noodle soup

Unbelievably fast and filling - unbelievably delicious.
We like ours with fresh challeh and butter.

Serves: 2
Prep time: 5 minutes
Cooking time: 10 minutes

Ingredients:
- one-half pound **regular tofu - fresh**
- chicken or vegetable bouillon to make 5 cups soup - use cubes <u>or</u>
  granules - we like Knorr brand but any kind is fine
- 1 tsp.onion powder - not onion salt
- 1/4 tsp.dry parsley
- 1 Tbls.oil - we use olive here - but canola is okay too
- 10 oz.Chinese style noodles - <u>or</u> egg noodles
- 1 cup frozen vegetables - peas – carrots – celery - parsnip
  - pea pods - use any combination
- *optional - 2 scallions - sliced into 1/4" pieces*
- *optional - 1/4 cup thin sliced mushrooms - fresh or canned*
- *optional - 2 tsp.butter or margarine - when using margarine*
  - we always use the non-hydrogenated kind with no trans-fatty acids

How to:
- pour 5 cups water into a 3 quart pot and turn burner to high
- add bouillon - onion powder - parsley and oil
- cut tofu into 1/2" cubes and add to pot
- add noodles - stir - bring back to boil - turn burner down
  to medium so the boil is not so vigorous - and cook
  2 minutes less than the noodle directions call for
- add vegetables - bring back to a boil – remove from heat
- *if you like you're soup richer - you can add*
  one tsp.butter or margarine to each bowl just
  before serving. We prefer getting the butter into the
  soup by dunking our bread.

Tomato ravioli zuppa

Open a few cans - heat - and presto you have a hearty delicious meal. We eat ours with hot garlic French bread on the side.
Serves: 4
Prep time: 10 minutes
Cooking time: 10 minutes

Ingredients:
- one pound **regular tofu - fresh**
- beef or vegetable bouillon cubes or granules – enough
  to make 4 cups - we like Knorr but any brand is fine
- 1/2 tsp.onion powder - not onion salt
- 1/2 tsp.garlic powder - not garlic salt
- one 14 oz.can diced tomatoes
- one 14 oz.can whole leaf spinach - drained
- two 15 oz.cans beef ravioli
- black pepper – we prefer fresh cracked
- 1 cup parmesan cheese

How to:
- pour 4 cups water into a large soup pot
- add bouillon - onion and garlic powders
- cut tofu into 1/2" cubes - add and bring to a boil
- add tomatoes - spinach and ravioli – and mix gently
  so as not to break up the tofu or ravioli
- bring back to a boil - turn down - cover - and
  simmer - 5 minutes
- garnish with fresh cracked pepper and lots of parmesan.

Lentil Swiss chard borsht

This is our favorite winter soup. It's best with a great loaf of whole wheat or black bread and butter.

Serves: 6
Prep time: 10 minutes
Cooking time: 40 minutes

Ingredients:
- one pound **regular tofu - fresh**
- beef or vegetable bouillon - enough to make 8 cups
  - we like Knorr bouillon but any brand is fine
- oil - we use olive here but canola will do
- 1 1/2 cups small French green lentils – <u>do</u> <u>not</u> use regular lentils
- 1 large yellow onion
- 3 cloves garlic
- 2 bunches red Swiss chard
- 1 bunch fresh cilantro
- 1 tsp.ground cumin
- 1/2 cup lemon juice - we like fresh squeezed
- fresh cracked black pepper
- course ground kosher sea salt for garnish

How to:
- pour 8 cups water in a large soup pot
- add bouillon and 2 Tbls.oil - bring to a boil
- pick over lentils - rinse and add to pot - bring back to
  a boil - turn down - cover and simmer - 20 minutes
- pour 2 Tbls.oil into 10" frying pan
- chop onion fine and sauté till soft and transparent
- add fine chopped garlic and sauté - 5 minutes - take
  off burner
- cut tofu into 1/2" cubes - add to soup pot - bring to a boil
- cut 1 inch of stem from chard and discard - wash leaves well
  - slice leaves and stems across into 1/2" pieces – add to soup pot
- bring back to boil - turn down - cover and simmer - 20 minutes
- during the last 5 minutes of cooking - using a spatula
  - scrape onions - garlic and all the pan juices into
  the lentils - stir in 1 cup chopped cilantro leaves -
  cumin - and 1/4 cup lemon juice – bring back to a boil
- serve garnished with pepper – kosher salt and finely
  chopped cilantro - and put the extra lemon juice on
  the table for those who want more.

New Orleans filé gumbo

This is absolutely marvelous with rice. We serve potato bread along side to sop-up every drop of the gorgeous sauce.
Serves: 4
Prep time: 10 minutes
Cooking time: 45 minutes

Ingredients:
- one pound **regular tofu - fresh**
- 2 Tbls.oil - we prefer extra virgin olive here
- 1 large yellow onion
- 3 stalks celery - the tender inner stalks
- 1 green pepper
- 2 medium cloves garlic
- 2 cups chicken or vegetable broth - use canned - cubes or granules -
  we prefer Knorr but any brand is fine
- one 14 oz.can diced tomatoes in juice
- one 10 oz.package frozen sliced okra
- 1/2 tsp.fresh ground chili paste
- 1/4 to 1/2 tsp.salt
- 1/2 tsp.fresh cracked pepper
- rice for 4 people - you may want to use the recipe on p.44
- *optional - 1 pound catfish - <u>or</u> one pound shelled and de-veined prawns*
- 1 tsp.filé gumbo

How to:
- pour oil into a large heavy bottomed soup pot or dutch oven
- chop onion - celery - green pepper and garlic and
  sauté till tender - about 10 minutes
- add broth - tomatoes - okra - chili paste - salt and pepper
- cut tofu into 1" cubes - add to pot
- bring to a boil - turn down - cover and simmer - 20 minutes
- make rice
- *if your are using catfish - add it to pot the last*
  10 minutes - check for bones - cut into 1"cubes – lay over vegetables
- *if you're using prawns - add them to pot the last 5 mniutes*
- sprinkle the filé gumbo spice into pot just before serving – and stir
  gently so as not to break up the tofu
- spoon rice onto one side of a deep plate - and gumbo onto the other.

Cabbage and noodles

Everyone loves this dish. We serve it with a plate of thin sliced oranges - fresh potato bread and butter.
Serves: 4
Prep time: 30 minutes
Cooking time: 30 minutes

Ingredients:
- one pound **regular tofu - fresh**
- 2 Tbls.oil - we use canola or corn here but olive is good too
- 1 large yellow onion - chopped
- 1 large clove garlic - minced
- chicken or vegetable bouillon - enough for 6 cups - cans
  - cubes or granules - we like Knorr but any brand is fine
- 1 tsp.wonton soup mix <u>or</u> 1 Tbls.Bragg's liquid aminos
- soy sauce - we prefer tamari
- 1/2 tsp.fresh ground chili paste - or more if you like
  it hot - we use 1/2 tsp.
- 1 nappa cabbage
- 1 bunch scallions
- 16 oz.Japanese udon noodles or the wider Chinese style noodles

How to:

- using a large heavy bottom soup pot - pour in oil and
  turn burner to medium
- add onion and stir-fry till soft - 5 minutes
- add garlic and cook - 1 minute
- add 6 cups water and bouillon cubes to pot - bring to
  a boil - mix to dissolve
- cut tofu into 1/2 inch cubes and add to pot
- add wonton soup mix <u>or</u> Bragg's aminos
- add 2 Tbls.soy sauce to chili paste - mix into pot
- cut nappa cabbage starting at leaf end into 1/4" slices
  - discarding last 2" of stalk
- cut scallions into 1" lengths
- add cabbage and scallions - bring to a boil - turn down
  - cover - simmer 10 minutes
- make noodles according to the package - when they're
  done - rinse and drain in a strainer
- divide noodles into large soup bowls and ladle on the soup
- and put the soy sauce on the table.

Veggie stew

Easy to make and so satisfying. We like to cook this stew on cold winter afternoon to heat-up the kitchen and send the aroma through the house. It refrigerates well - and re-heats easily in the microwave. We serve it with fresh bread and butter - any fresh bread works here.

Serves: 4
Prep time: 20 minutes
Cooking time: 40 minutes

Ingredients:
- one pound **firm tofu - fresh**
- 2 Tbls.oil - we use walnut oil here but olive or canola is okay
- 1 large yellow onion - chopped
- 1 tsp.dry parsley
- 1/2 tsp.dry rosemary - crushed
- 1 bunch scallions - cut into 1/2" lengths
- 1/2 pound mushrooms sliced thin - or one 4 oz.can sliced
- 2 cups cauliflower or broccoli or 1 cup each - fresh or frozen
- 2 medium-large russet baking potatoes cut into 1/2" cubes
- 2 large cloves garlic - minced
- 1/2 tsp.black pepper - we prefer fresh cracked
- 1 tsp.sugar
- 2 packages dry soup mix - we use onion-mushroom but onion
  or beefy-onion or one of each is good too
- butter or margarine - we only use margarine that is non-
  hydrogenated and had no trans-fatty acids
- garnish salt – we like course ground kosher salt for this

How to:
- pour oil into a large heavy bottomed soup pot and
  turn burner to medium
- add onion - sauté - 10 minutes
- add garlic - stir-fry - one minute
- pour in 6 cups water and bring to boil
- add parsley - rosemary - soup mix - and pepper - mix well
- cut tofu into 1/2" cubes and add
- bring back to boil - turn down - simmer - 10 minutes
- add cauliflower - broccoli and potatoes - simmer 10 minutes
- add scallions and simmer 5 minutes - check potatoes and
  vegetables with a fork to make sure they're soft - if not
  simmer 5 more minutes
- serve in large bowls garnished with a tsp.butter - salt and pepper.

Creamy potato leek soup

Leeks have a wonderful flavor all their own - and they're tender and plentiful in the fall - a good time for soup. We love this recipe - and serve it as a main course with fresh dark rye bread and butter.

Serves: 4
Prep time: 30 minutes
Cooking time: 40 minutes

Ingredients:
- 10-14 oz.**soft silken tofu - fresh**
- 7 cups vegetable bouillon broth - cubes - cans or granules
  - we use Knorr **-** but any brand is fine
- 3 Tbls.oil - we like walnut but olive or canola is okay
- 1 large clove garlic minced <u>or</u> 1/2 tsp.garlic powder
- 1/4 tsp.rosemary
- 1/4 tsp.cumin
- 1/8 tsp.cayenne pepper
- 1/4 to 1/2 tsp.salt – and try course ground kosher salt here for garnish
- 1 tsp.sugar
- 2 medium-size leeks
- 2 large or 3 medium-size russet baking potatoes
- 1 cup whole milk
- butter or margarine - when we use margarine - it's always
  the non-hydrogenated kind with no trans-fatty acids
- black pepper to garnish - fresh ground is best

How to:
- pour 7 cups bouillon into a large heavy bottomed soup pot
  and turn burner to medium
- add oil - garlic - spices and sugar - bring to a boil
- trim both ends of the leeks and discard - now cut
  down the center from white to green - sand likes
  to hide inside – especially where the white meets the green - so
  immerse in cold water - wash well and inspect - now slice
  crosswise into 1/4" pieces and add to pot
- skin potatoes - cut into 1/2" cubes - add
- bring pot back to a boil - turn down - cover - simmer - 30 minutes
- remove 2 cups of soup from pot and set aside
- cut tofu into large cubes - add to pot
- pour in milk
- now using a hand-held blender - purée the soup right in the
  pot till tofu and vegetables are completely blended
- add the un-blended soup back into pot - heat 10 minutes
- serve bowls garnished with 1 tsp.butter - a sprinkle
  of course kosher salt and fresh-cracked black pepper.

Velvet lima bean soup

This is beautiful soup - we love it's luscious texture - and serve it with crustini - fresh brown or rye bread and butter - or if you're feeling ambitious - buy a box of matzo meal - make some matzo balls and float 2 or 3 in each bowl.

Serves: 6
Prep time: 40 minutes + soaking beans overnight
Cooking time: 80 minutes

Ingredients:
- 10-14 oz.**soft silken tofu - fresh**
- 1 (16 oz.) package dried large lima beans
- 1 large yellow onion
- 4 large mushrooms
- 3 Tbls.oil - we prefer olive here but canola is okay
- 6 cups vegetable or chicken bouillon - from cans - cubes or
  granules - we use Knorr but any brand will do
- 1/2 cup orange or brown lentils
- 1 tsp.dill
- 1/2 to 3/4 tsp.salt
- 1/4 tsp.pepper - we always use fresh cracked
- 2 large russet baking potatoes – we like Idaho potatoes
- 1 cup milk – whole – skim or soy
- 1 Tbls.lemon juice
- butter or margarine - if we use margarine - we only use
  the non-hydrogenated kind with no trans-fatty acids

How to:
- before going to bed - pick over beans - place in a 6 to 8
  quart pot - add 8 cups water - bring to a boil - take off
  burner and leave covered over-night
- the skins should have split open - drain the beans in a
  strainer - now pop the skins off by rolling each one
  between thumb and fingers - discard skins
- put beans back in pot - add 6 cups water
- now - chop onion and mushrooms - sauté in oil till brown - don't
  hurry - well-browned onion is essential to the flavor
- add to soup pot - using a spatula to scrape the frying pan clean
- add bouillon - dill - salt and pepper to pot
- add lentils
- peel and cut potatoes into 1" cubes and add
- bring to a boil – stir - turn down to low - cover and
  simmer till the limas have disintegrated - about 1 hour
- cut tofu into 1" cubes - add to pot
- pour in milk and lemon juice
- using a hand held blender - puree soup till smooth as velvet
- heat on low - 15 minutes
- spoon in large bowls with serve with 1 tsp.butter melting on top.

TOFU NOW INDEX

Join NOW or give a gift membership. Make sure the new member's name and address is complete and spelled correctly.

NOW Membership Application

Count me in! I wish to join NOW and commit myself to take action to bring women into full participation in the mainstream of American society now, exercising all privileges and responsibilities thereof in truly equal partnership with men.

_____
Name (please print)

_____
Street Address

_____
City/State/Zip

_____
Phone   E-mail

Please check your choice:
[ ]Regular dues. $35 covers national, state and local dues:
    $40 for residents of AZ, CA, CT, IL, IN, MI, NY.

[ ]Reduced Dues. A sliding scale available from $15 to $34.

[ ]Check enclosed payable to NOW   *Check number_____

[ ]MasterCard   [ ]VISA   [ ]AMEX

Card number_____Exp.Date_____

Cardholder Name_____

Signature_____

WHERE TO FIND US:
National Organization for Women
733 15th Street NW, 2nd Floor
Washington, DC 20005
Phone: (202) 628-8669
FAX: (202) 785-8576
E-mail: now@now.org
Internet: www.now.org

Photocopies of this page accepted.

TOFU NOW ORDER FORM

TOFU NOW by Susan Lebow
A National Organization for Women Cookbook

Online order: www.now.org/catalog - orders are placed using a credit card
Phone order: 1-800-507-7007 (from 10 to 6 Mon-Fri.) - **orders are placed using a credit card**
Fax: 301-731-6101 - for VISA/MC and American Express credit card orders ONLY - (Please include ship to and contact information)

for UPS Delivery Order: (we ship UPS so please provide your street address)
Date_____
Name_____
(please print)
Street Delivery Address _____
(for UPS delivery)
City/State/Zip_____

Daytime Phone _____ **E-mail**_____
(PLEASE give your phone/e-mail in case we have questions)

Your Order	Quantity	Total
TOFU NOW - BK-TN - @ $19.95 ea.		$
Shipping & Handling (see below)		$
Total		$

Shipping & Handling
 Chart for UPS/USPS*
$15.00 to $30.00 $6.95
$30.01 to $45.00 $7.95
$45.01 to $60.00 $8.95
$60.01 to $75.00 $9.95
$75.01 to $100.00 $10.95
Over $100: $10.95 + 5% of amount over $100
DC resident tax 6% if applicable
* International orders must pay by credit card and will be charged international UPS postage rates.

[ ] **MasterCard**   [ ] **VISA**   [ ] **AMEX**
[ ] **Check** enclosed payable to **NOW** Products   **Check number**_____
Account Number_____**Expiration Date**_____
Cardholder Name_____
Signature_____

Mail order form and payment to:
NOW
733 15th Street NW, 2nd Floor
Washington, DC 20005
DON'T SEND CASH   Photocopies of this page accepted.

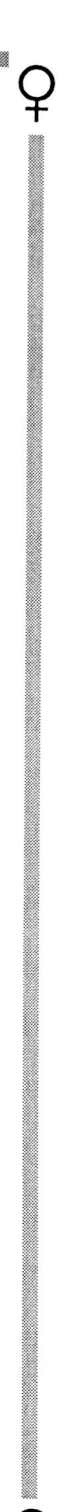